I Choose to Go on Singing

Ada Mae Harper, 2006

Ada Mae Harper

VIP
VISION IMPRINTS PUBLISHING
A Thomas Nelson Company

www.thomasnelson.com
Tulsa, Oklahoma

I CHOOSE TO GO ON SINGING
© 2006 by Ada Mae Harper

Vision Imprints Publishing, Inc.
8801 S. Yale, Suite 410
Tulsa, OK 74137
918-493-1718

Unless otherwise noted, all Scripture quotations are
taken from the King James Version of the Bible.

ISBN 1-599510-07-3
Library of Congress catalog card number: 2005937028
Printed in the United States of America

Dedication

To my children, grandchildren
and great grandchildren:
My prayer is that they may choose
to stay so full of God
that they will rise up with eagle wings and
keep the victory through their greatest trials.
I love them so much!

Contents

Foreword

When you're sitting in the hospital, not sure whether your child is going to live or die and then the telephone rings. The woman on the other end of the phone has a word from the Lord. This word carries you through the next few days of tests and on to recovery. You are having one of those days when nothing is going right and you are worried about issues at home. You go to the mail box and find a card full of just the right words for the right moment. You have a big project at work and the boss is expecting you to make it happen. The pressure is great and you remember you have to return a couple of e-mails. When you open your inbox, there, in the box is an e-card with just the right encouragement, prayer or confidence booster that you need.

This is how my life has been since I can remember. Having a mother that knew when, where and what I needed even before I knew I needed it. She was not always physically able to be by my side. But, she was with me through every trial, every victory and every success as she put pen to paper and followed the leading of the Lord.

This book is a collection of some of the words of encouragement that she has shared with our family, grocery clerks, waitresses, doctors, lab technicians, nurses, etc. Many times I have watched as she would be eating dinner with my family. Mom would excuse herself and walk across the restaurant to someone God put on her heart. She sometimes prayed with them or spoke a few encouraging words. Mom always left a printed poem in their hands.

I know this book is divinely inspired by the Lord. I pray that it will give someone, somewhere, inspiration or consolation at a time of need. Ada Harper's life and these words are proof that Jesus truly is our comfort. He is willing and able to guide us through all the storms of life as we "Choose to Go on Singing".

I love you, Mom and I'm proud to be your daughter.

Donna deBlois

Preface

We live in a world of so much pain and hurt. Our attitudes and choices each day cause us to live or just exist. I do not want (nor have I ever wanted) to just exist. My desire is to live a fruitful, productive life in spite of any circumstance or quality of life around me.

The Lord brought me back from sure death many years ago and gave me this promise: "I shall not die, but live, and declare the works of the Lord". Psalm 118:17

I have walked through many painful experiences. Some of these are: a loss of a baby, an epileptic son, financial trauma, cancer in my body (from which God healed me 53 years ago) and the loss of my husband of 45 years. Sometimes my song lay dormant for a few days. But, then it always came forth with new vigor as I regained my focus and looked to the Lord.

This book comes from my heart felt convictions. These writings came during quiet times, in prayer, at public gatherings and in worship with Jesus. The inspirations on the following pages are being offered as words of comfort and help to all who need His touch.

God in me, and the joy He gives, is the source of my strength. He receives all the glory for my happiness and peace. For, He is, and will always be, my first love. Therefore, my choice is this: "**I Choose** to go on singing"! I do love Him so!

Circumstances will not, or cannot, turn you back "as you keep on singing".

Acknowledgments

Throughout the seventy seven years of my life, my family and many friends supported me. Over the years, these individuals continually encouraged the publishing of my poems. I wish to thank each one for their consistent prayers, confidence and love. They helped to make this book a reality.

Thanks to my daughter, Lynda Noland, for the long hours of research and dedication in getting the material ready for publication.

Above all, I thank my Heavenly Father for the inspiration and words He gave to me to share with you.

I Choose To Go On Singing

There's a choice we must make
In the mainstream of life
Every day, whatever its bringing
We can walk in our misery
Imagined or real
Live our life by the way we feel
Or, we can choose to go on singing

The uncertainties, the heartaches,
The grief and the pain
May cross our pathway
Again and again
The rain will fall
The sun won't shine
The certainty of death
The shortness of time

So many things will come today
But we can choose, no matter the test
To put our trust in God and know His sweet rest
Lift our head and go on singing

Jesus is our friend
He will not fail
Whatever the day may be bringing
Whatever may come
How dark it may seem
I Choose To Go On Singing

If we can do nothing about 'it'
We have two options:
Wallow in our 'misery' or
Go singing on our way
I Choose To Go On Singing

My Choice

I choose to go on singing
I choose to lighten my day
I choose to go on singing
To roll the dark clouds away

I choose to go on singing
While others lay down to die
I choose to go on singing
Instead of always asking 'why'

Our Great God has all the answers
He knows what He's doing with me
I choose to go on singing
And not question His Great Diety

This Minute

Let's bless the world with a smile
Let's bless the world with His Spirit
Let's bless the world with all we have
This Minute!

Let's bless the world with His presence
Let's bless the world with His power
Let's bless the world with what we have in our hand
This Minute!

Give and it shall be given unto you
Is a spiritual law of His Word
As we give, it shall be returned to us
Accordingly as we have heard
Not in kind, necessarily, but abundantly
This Minute!

Though I Walk

Yea, though I walk
Through the valley of death
I know that He holds my hand
Yea, though the waters swirl around me
I know I'll be able to stand

Many be the afflictions of the righteous
But Jesus delivers and brings us through
He will not allow
The rivers to overflow us
His grace is sufficient
His strength ever new

We are able, in Him, to do all things
Whatever those things may be
We can know His assurance and blessing
Although our eyes cannot, as yet, see

We will walk through this day
We will trust, though we don't understand
We will rejoice through all of our tears
And know He's working His plan

We'll listen for His voice of direction
We'll hold steady in His silence and wait
For He will, and does, hear the cry of our heart
His answer is never too late!

The Power of His Presence

By The Power of His Presence
We have the Victory!

By The Power of His Presence
All Things will be!

By The Power of His Presence
We rejoice in the storm!

By The Power of His Presence
We're safe from all harm!

By The Power of His Presence
The future looks bright!

By The Power of His Presence
As we walk in the Light!

Good Morning

In the coolness of the morning
When the mists have rolled away
And the sun peaks out to say hello
And welcome the new day

Your heart is free from worry
Your body fresh and new
Your soul and spirit singing
It's a new beginning in everything you do

There is a glorious expectancy
For the happenings of the day
It really doesn't matter
If you're at work or play

The hand of God is moving
And you know that "All is well"
You're rejoicing and you're happy
And you've the whole world to tell

Be Happy Anyway

It does no good to cry and pout
It does no good to fuss and fret
It does no good to doubt
For you're the one in misery!

It does no good to be at odds
With all of those around you
Even though they disagree
Let God's peace surround you

It does no good to be unhappy
And complain about the day
For this is the day the Lord has made
So be happy anyway!

First Step

The road may be long
Twisting and uphill
Can't see very far ahead
Tempted to stand still

But our journey is waiting
For us to make a start
We must consider well
And take the first step

Not looking back
We will reach our goal
In time
His time

The most important step is
The first one!

Who's Old?

A wrinkle here, a wrinkle there
A tiny bald spot, a few white hairs
Is this supposed to mean we're old?
That seems to be the thing we're told

But life is just now rich and good
Somehow we're thinking as we should
Our wisdom has increased with each year
We've learned the things we should hold dear

We've learned to lay our burden down
How to smile and not to frown
To be thankful for each day we live
Not to be takers, but the joy to give

To be old is mostly in our mind
So I think I'll leave that thought behind
And walk each day on up the road
And refuse to bear that heavy load
That I'm getting old

I Can!

There is absolutely nothing
In this world I cannot do
If I hold His hand
Walk in His plan
And to His Word be true

There is absolutely nothing
That He requires of me
Where His grace
Is not sufficient
For what I need to be

I Can! I Will!

If

I Want To!

Today

Today is the day which the Lord hath made
A truth we cannot ignore
We must rejoice and be glad in it
And lay aside all the days gone before

Tomorrow is so very uncertain
For we know not what it may bring
Today is here, the Lord hath made it
Let's lift our hearts and sing

Let's do the good things
That our heart cries to do
Let's say the kind words
To lift other folk too

Let's enjoy the Lord's presence
No kindness too small
Not put off till tomorrow
And do nothing at all

Today is the day
Which the Lord hath made
We'll trust in Him
And not be afraid

We'll walk in His presence
Let His love shine through
And let Him use us
As He wants to do

Tomorrow is uncertain
We don't know what it will bring
So, today is the day
To let our heart sing

Thankful

I have so much to be thankful for
As I count my blessings today
I'm rich in the things God provides me
And I'm glad that I walk in this way

I will have all sufficiency in all things
That I may share as I go
This is His promise of blessing
And He will not fail me, I know!

As I give forth of all His provisions
That He has entrusted to me
He will continually fill my baskets
And a blessing to others I'll be

I Can - Today

Today I can be happy
Today I can sing and shout
Today I can let His sunshine
Drive away my fears and doubts

Today I can share His blessings
Today I can believe on His Name
Today I can show forth His love
And today I'll not be the same

Those around me will certainly see it
Although they may not comprehend
Today your Spirit in me
Will touch the hearts of men

If

'If is such a tiny word
But as I look around and see
I understand the great effect
It can have on me

'If surely is a condition
'If surely brings a choice
'If is almost the strongest word
Uttered by the human voice

'If hides all my excuses
And all of my failures too
"If things had only been different"
Or "if it hadn't been for you"

"If I only had a million
You'd see what I would do"
"If you would just agree with me
I know the Lord would too"

'If can bring on the victory
'If we will go the right way

For Jesus said
"If you abide in Me
I'll be with you always
If you have seen Me
You've seen the Father too
If you ask anything in My Name
I will surely give it to you"

'If has only two little letters
It's very small, you see
It's up to me what great effect

'If

Has on me

Tomorrow

When we're planning
Only for tomorrow
And lose track of today
We're never happy or contented
Just miserable all the way

We miss the blessings of the present
We're always saying 'when'
We feel we are failing all the time
And see only 'what might have been'

When we're planning only for tomorrow
Reaching for the things that 'soon will be'
The time we have runs quickly by
And so does victory

So let's trust God for our tomorrow
Leave behind what 'might have been'
Looking forward with great expectancy
Not wondering 'where' or 'when'

Knowing God, who gave the promise
Always does just what He said
We'll then be happy on our journey
Moving on toward things ahead

You Can Do It

You can do it
Oh! Yes you can
The greatest of challenges
It's part of His plan

He never requests anything
That you cannot do
With His help and direction
He'll see you through

You can do it
Oh! Yes you can
As you listen closely
And follow His plan

Keep Your Chin Up!

Keep your chin up
Keep on walking
In the sunlight of His love
It's impossible
To hang your head down
When you're looking up above

Keep your chin up
Keep on singing
Moving in His power and love
It's impossible
To hang your head down
When you're looking up above

The Eyes of A Child

If I could only see
Through the eyes of a child
How simple life would be
The beauty of the rainbow
The buzz of a bee
The fluffy white clouds in the sky
Would fascinate me

The flowers on the roadside
The rocks on the shore
The frogs in the pond
Spider web on the door

If I could only see
Through the eyes of a child
How beautiful and simple
Life would be

The Day Before Tomorrow

The day before tomorrow
Is the day that I should do it
The day before tomorrow
I really must get to it

The day before tomorrow
Challenges every bit of me
For the day before tomorrow
Is really today, you see

Courage

It takes a lot of courage
Strength and a made up mind
To see the high mountain ahead
And decide you're going to climb

Not to be discouraged
By circumstances and pain
Not to lie down
Feel sorry for yourself
But stand tall and try again

It takes a special person
And I know that you are one
To climb to the top of the mountain
And see a job well done

I Know The Lord

I know the Lord
He leadeth me
By the still waters
The deep rolling sea
In pastures green
In deserts dry
In darkness of night
Sun high in the sky

I know the Lord
He leadeth me
In valleys low
Over mountains steep
And holds me close
While I am asleep
I know the Lord

We Will Yet Praise You

When the clouds hang low
The storm rages
We've no place to go
We will yet praise you, Lord

When pain cries out
In the midnight hour
No relief in sight
We will look to the morning
And know things will be better
And we will praise you, Lord

When loneliness hugs us
Like a blanket
We wish only for the touch of a hand
We remember your words
"I'll not leave you alone"
And we will praise you, Lord

He Gives Me Peace

You have given me peace
In the midst of my storm
Though fierce winds did blow
You kept me from harm

You have given me peace
And great joy within
Though strong be the battle
You kept me from sin

You have given me peace
There could be no doubt
You were loosing my chains
And bringing me out

You have given me peace
None can take it away
I'm standing up tall
This is a new day

The Greatest of Mornings

I looked forward to today
And slept through the night
I knew whatever I had to face
Would turn out alright

For I have seen many times before
The day would be
How I expected it to go
And how it would affect me

So I turned it over to the Lord
Because He is in control
He is my Savior and my friend
The keeper of my soul

Life Is What You Make It

Life is what you make it
Is my thought for you today
We can carry all the burdens
Or let them at the altar lay

We can moan and groan and complain
Let tears run down our face
Or walk on this road of life
Happy, by His amazing grace

It matters not to others
How deep our pain may be
They only are affected
By what they hear and see

We cannot be discouraged
Knowing they do not understand
But let the light of Jesus shine
And do the best we can

The Quiet Place

There is a 'Quiet', Lord
That goes beyond the lack of noise
The 'Quiet' in the inner chambers of my heart
As I sit in reverence to hear
What you have to say to me

I only understand with my spiritual heart
And hear with my spiritual ears
As I sit there, the world is shut out
Nothing really matters
I come away refreshed
Renewed and at peace

Grant that I will find my way there often
And reach out to share this
'Quiet' with others

"Be still and know that I am God"

Counting Blessings

I stopped to count my blessings
I found an impossible task
For every one I counted
Seemed to multiply so fast

I thanked God for health and strength
And all the things He helped me do
Then I started to remember
The many hard places He helped me through

I thanked Him for others
Who had warmed and touched my way
Then I remembered the little things
That had truly made my day

I thanked Him
That He came in love
And gave His life for me
Then I remembered what he purchased
At Calvary

Beginnings of Thanksgiving

I am thankful for the morning
For in it, I have a fresh beginning
A new day
A glorious opportunity
I am thankful

I am thankful
I can open my eyes and see
The beauty of the mist in the trees
The grass and the flowers
The smile of a baby
The wrinkled hand of one
Who walked this way before me

I am thankful
I can hear with my ears
The noise of a new day
The chirp of a bird, whir of a bee
The music of God as He tunes
The instruments of my soul
My name being called
By someone who loves me

I am thankful
I can use my voice
To speak words of love and encouragement
To praise and sing unto my God
To call my little grandchild's name
To share with others
To communicate
I am thankful

Life

Life is fleeting
Today we are here
Tomorrow we are gone
In the spring
We shoot up as little sprouts
Live through the summer
Then comes winter
And we are gone
Never to be seen again in this life
Only memories
Good or bad

We have touched lives
Many through our seasons
God grant we made a difference for good
To all those we passed by
That their lives will be better
As they walk on through
The spring
The summer
And winter
Of their lives

Oh God!!!

To live the life
From day to day
Showing others by how I live
The Way

Believing your Word
In every circumstance and pain
Knowing victory is already mine
I'll smile again

Looking only for good
In all I see and meet
No condemnation in my heart
Laying everything
At His feet

Singing and making melody in my heart
Praying always
Giving thanks in all things
Walk with my hand in His
To do my part

To touch the lives
Of others every day
When He speaks
To be willing to go
Or to stay

To lay my head
On my pillow at night
To know sweet peace
Because I did obey
To be a living sacrifice
Wholly acceptable
In His sight

This Day Holds The Simple Things

Hearing the quietness of the morning
Feeling the warmth of the
Sun on my face
Taking time to say 'hello'
To my neighbor

Looking inside myself
Finding my place
Seeing God in everything
That touches my life
Realizing He is watching
And guiding me
That I will be a blessing
To others every day
As I gently open my heart
And let Him have His way

Not fretting because I cannot do
The physical things I once could
But rest in Him
Let Him guide
My hands, my feet
And strengthen me
As he said He would

Only One

There is only one way to go
There is only one place to be
To be walking in God's will and spirit
Eternally

There is only one word to hear
There is only one thing to do
Move in the power of His spirit
As He speaks to you

I Will Go On

I cannot stop
I cannot quit
I still have a future
There is yet a candle to be lit
That it might shine
Into some darkened space
And keep someone from falling

I cannot quit
I cannot fear
For there are those waiting
In the valley of decision
For a helping hand
A listening ear

I will not lie down
In the midst of grief and pain
Saying "I have nothing to give
Nothing to gain, I am finished"
When I know that God
Is yet the same

He Is Leading

I cannot see
I cannot know
Every step I take
Or place I'm to go

But I am sure
He leads the way
As I obey Him
Every day

I will not stumble
I will not fall
I'll hold His hand
And stand up tall

He knows my future
He made the plan
He will lead me onward
Help me to stand

Give me grace
Through every trial
Put a song in my heart
On my face a smile

So I will trust Him
No matter the test
Leave it all in His hands
For He knows best

Three Rosebuds In The Night

My heart was aching
Filled with pain
The works I was doing
Seemed all in vain

I was hurrying
Here and there
Praying as I went
Doing my best to share

Somehow it suddenly
Seemed so fruitless
It wasn't doing any good
No one really seemed to care

Then I received
Three rosebuds in the night

A knock came at the door
So soft I could hardly hear
A tiny brown eyed angel stood there
A bright smile on his little face

"Special Delivery" he said
As he handed me
Three rosebuds
Tucked in a vase

You've Been Here Before

You've been here
Many times before
And every time
God's opened the door

When weary and tired
He's given rest
In all the temptations
You've stood the test

With your pain
Came the healer
With hunger
The food

In darkness
The light shining through
In your weakness
Came strength as your day

In confusion
Peace from above
In times of loneliness
You've felt the greatest of love

Ada Mae Harper

He's Standing By

In the midst of hurt
And deepest pain
There is 'One'
Who standeth by
Until your world
Is upright again
Until the tears
You shed are dry
There is 'One'
That 'standeth by'

When darkness is so thick
No rays of sun to shine
The valley is so deep
The mountains high
No place to lean
Your head and cry
He's 'standing by'

When the sun comes out
With glorious rays of light
The brightness pushed away the night
Everything is fresh and new
You begin again, to do
All the things you wanted to
Don't forget
He's 'standing by'

Look! Here! Know!

The beautiful waves of the ocean
The salty white sands along the shore
The puffy cotton clouds in the blue sky
Oh, who could ask for more

The dew drops on the grass in the morning
As the sun rises up for the day
The flowers sleepily opening their eyes
The little squirrels happy and gay

The music of the birds in the tree tops
As they awake, the great day to greet
The sounds of the laughter of children
The expressions on their faces so sweet

Oh yes, let's rejoice in this day
Our Creator has made it so
Let's not miss
These glorious blessings

Let us look!

Let us hear!

Let us know!

My Cry

Oh God, I will praise You
With all that I am
And then all I can be
Will come about
As your fullness
Is brought forth in me

My cry is
To be like you
Powerful, compassionate
Free from all hindrances
Abundantly able
To give all of myself
So others may see in me
Only Thee

Like Thee

Oh to see
Oh to hear
Oh to do
Oh to be
Like Thee!

"I will bless you
Cause My face
To shine upon you
And give you peace"

To Trust

To trust is a must
To receive
We believe

If we 'Be'
We will see
God's blessings

56

Eagle Wings

God not only gives us peace and joy
In the midst of the storms
But eagle wings
So that in the midst of it all
We can rise and see
Our future is still out there

Upside Down

When things go upside down
The sun is behind the clouds
There is the fact
That the greatest things
Have not changed
Just those things that we know
Will be better tomorrow
Or the next day

Lord, My Desire

Let my life touch the lives of others
Wherever they may be
Your anointing that is within me
Will make a difference
Wherever I may be

Let me light up a darkened room
By your power that lives in me
Let broken hearts be mended
Blinded eyes to see

Let your glory overcome all obstacles
As you reign in your great majesty
And wherever I go
Whatever I do
For others to see only thee

Others May See

I want to walk in your spirit
Sing forth your praise
Manifest your power
In all of my ways

Let the aura of your presence
Shine forth in my face
So that others may see you
As I run this race

My walk in obedience
Will show them the way
Lighten their heavy burdens
Turn darkness to day

This I Know

I do not know
I cannot see
Every step I take
But there's victory
Because my Lord
He leadeth me
This I know!

Desire

The things that you desire
Are still waiting
To fall at your feet
In due time

As you move
In My strength
And power
To set men free

The desires
Of your heart
Will come
To be

It Is Mine!

There is no doubt about it
I know God has heard my prayer
Now I can sing and shout it
As I've laid on Him my care

Though as yet I may not see it
I am sure the answer belongs to me
For I've taken hold of His promise
It will surely come to be

For He said, if we would ask
And upon His name believe
That whatsoever I desire
That I would receive

God is not a man that He should lie
And He never makes a mistake
Not one word of His promise
Will He ever forsake!

I Cannot Help But Praise You!

I cannot help but praise You
In the darkest of the night
I close my eyes in shadows
And open them to the light

I cannot help but praise You
As I start into this day
For the darkest of the shadows
In your sunlight, have rolled away

I cannot help but praise You
Though the path I may not see
For I have a calm assurance
That you're walking there with me

Praise You, Jesus!

To Hear

To hear you, Lord
And only you
To obey you, Lord
In all I want to do

We seek so hard
To gain the approval of men
We forget that it is you
Before whom we stand

In the glory of your presence
By the power in your Name
I want to move
Only at your command

The Little Acorn

The Little Acorn
Fell to the ground
Imbedded itself
In the moist leaves and soil
It died

New life sprang up
A huge tree
Came to be
And from that
A little acorn fell
Life goes on eternally

His Way

I don't understand the reasons
Nor do I know the whys
But I know deep in my soul
That God is ever wise

The things that cross our pathway
The difficulties that we face
When put together with God's great plan
Always have a place

They fit the great puzzle of our life
In a special, perfect way
If in the midst of turmoil and pain
We let Him have His way!

Romans 8:28

A Gift For You

Oh weary, thirsty pilgrim
Pressed by sin and woe
I have a place of comfort
A place for you to go

I have a cup of cool water
A crust of bread to share
I have a light for your darkness
It all awaits you there

You'll find it wrapped in beauty
In love and compassion too
A bundle of joy and peace so sweet
Awaiting the bowing of your knee
To pick it up at Jesus' feet

My Aim

To walk with God alone
And hold His hand
To live in His presence
Though folks don't understand

To hear His sweet voice
Through all noise and clatter
Let Him be my choice
In all things that matter

To hold my head high
Walk on through the fight
So that my feet don't stumble
I'll let Him be the Light

My strength and my hope
Though the way may seem long
He lightens my burden
And gives me His song

Awake

Awake, oh soul
For the day is dawning
Awake and live
In this glorious day

Awake, oh soul
For it is morning
The darkness of night
Has passed away

Open your eyes
To the glories of the Lord
Let His praises
Ring out all the day

Stay your mind
Upon Him
Receive only His peace
And let Him clear the way

Our Hiding Place

As the eagle soars above the high mountains
And finds a place to nest
So as you walk in My spirit
You find a place of rest

The predators are there in the crevices
But the sharp eye of the eagle does see
Our enemies may surround us
But in His spirit we flee

As the eagle soars in the bright blue sky
Above any harm that may be near
We, as we walk in God's spirit
Have nothing to fear

The Source

I cannot tell you about it
For I really don't know the reason why
But there is one thing I can tell you
I know where the answers lie

There's a rock that's strong to stand on
There's an arm on which we can lean
There's an anchor in roughest of waters
A love beyond anything seen

He will change your life completely
As you trust Him and believe on His name
For Jesus has all your answers
And you never will be the same

My Sincere Prayer

Oh! God, deliver me from being a complainer
I don't wish it ever to be so
I want to shed joy, happiness
Contentment and peace
In every place that I go

Let me walk in such a manner
That my life will please you in every way
The thoughts of my mind, heart and spirit
Will glorify you as I
Do everything that you say

I want only to be thankful
And praise you
In the hardest of trial and pain
Though I may not understand at the moment
I will not murmur and complain

The Key

As we keep His commandments
And follow His ways
The blessings of heaven
Will fill up our days

Our treasure house and baskets
Will be full to overflow
Wherever we are needed
We'll be able to go

We can share in His spirit
And bless in His name
The place where we're standing
Will not be the same

As we keep His commandments
And follow His ways
The blessings of heaven
Will fill up our days

Deuteronomy 28:12-14

He Is The Same

There comes a time in all of our lives
When the world seems upside down
No one really understands or cares
Or so 'the whispers' come

But in spite of the enemy's whispers
Or his blatant booming voice
We know the Victor
And the victories
Are still the same
As when we made our choice

We're standing firm
We're holding still
In the midst of everything
God has not failed
He will not fail
He's ever more the same

His Presence

When I recognize His presence
Become aware that He is here
I have a peace that passes all understanding
I have not a single fear

I feel so strong, yet weaker
Than I've ever been before
My heart is filled with so much love
There seems no room for more

When I recognize His presence
That lives inside of me
There's no circumstance or happening
That can take my victory

"In His presence is fullness of joy"

Don't Give Up

Don't give up in the midst of the battle
Don't quit when the victory is near
Let My power flow out through your life
Keep your ears open to hear

If you give up when things look impossible
Who's going to deliver those in need
I've given you a field of labor
A place to sow My seed

Wait before Me, know My power
Then move to set men free
You can do it, I am with you
So let it be!

New Life

I waited on my knees that day
Knowing not just what to say
I didn't understand my burden
But it wouldn't go away

I lifted up my eyes to Him
He saw my need and then
My burden quickly rolled away
He forgave me all my sin

No words could then describe the peace
That came into my soul
I felt new life surge through my veins
As Jesus took control

Every Day Is A Gift

I opened my eyes this morning
And saw the rain
I crawled back under the covers
And closed them again

Then I sat with a start and remembered
I have this day before me
Another I might not see
So I started my day with a song
Glad that I could be

If I Can

If I can be a blessing
I'm useful, yes, indeed!
If I can warm the cold
And bread, the hungry feed

If I can be a blessing
By holding to a hand
By standing up
By being there
Doing the best I can

If I can yet do these things
Showing others that I care
My life is still of value
As I give of my best to share

Sing In The Battle

You told me to sing in the battle
You told me to trust in your Name
You told me to lean not to my understanding
You told me to trust in your Name

You said "Look not to the battle
But look to the victory"
You told me to sing in the battle
And stand in awe and see

You told me to sing in the battle
Wipe away the tears from my eyes
Walk forth in power and glory
And there I would see the prize

You told me to sing in the battle
Put my trust in you always
You told me to sing in the battle
And I would see the end of these days

Feelings

Sometimes you probably feel
No one cares or knows your needs
Then other times you feel
Like a 'flower' among the weeds

Sometimes you feel you're different
Than all of those you know
Then other times you feel
Like a clown on a TV show

But you are pretty special
There's no one quite like you
So remember that
Keep your chin up
Whatever others do!

His Sunlight

I waited in the shadows
Till the long, long day was through
I was waiting for the answer
Or just what I should do
I walked into His sunlight
And suddenly I could see
The answer lay before my eyes
It was waiting there for me

Ada Mae Harper

Look Up Higher

I walked today
Along a road strewn with garbage
And thought of the sin of the world

I raised my eyes a little higher
I saw the trees
The blue sky
The flowers
The fluffy white clouds
And thought of God

Look up higher
There is hope
There is beauty
There is God!

To Have A Grateful Heart

The greatest gift
You can give yourself
Is to have a grateful heart
When others complain
About the rain
You have sunshine
Your day to start

You're thankful for
The day ahead
The night that just has been
You know no matter
What may happen
You've victory at the end

Let It Be Me

Let me be the oil in the hinge
Sugar in the tea
Whatever is needed
Let it be me

As people stand on the ledge
Of indecision and pain
As hearts are broken
With nothing to gain

As their world is dark
They don't know where to go
Let me be the light
God's greatness to show

Let the warmth of your presence
Enfold them in peace
Feel your arms around them
As you give sweet release

Believe 'In' God

Believe 'in' God
Not just 'about' God
Not just 'what' He has done

I believe God formed the earth
Caused the sun and moon to be
Opened the Red Sea
Arose from the grave
But, I've got to believe
What He did for me

Believe 'in' God
Not just believe that He is
And can do anything He chooses
But that He will and has
Chosen the path, this day
This plan for me

Believe

The Glory of the Lord
Is hovering about this day
The birds are singing
The azaleas blooming
The sun is shining
Cool breezes blowing
How can we not believe

All things work together for good
To them who are called
To His purpose

Our Day

We truly make our day
From morning to night
As we march into victory
Or choose to fight

"The battle is mine"
Saith the Lord
"Give me your battles
And stand in My might
Your sun can be shining
Though others have rain
Trust Me, believe Me
And stand on My Name"

If I Think I Can

If I think I can
I surely will
If I think I can't
I won't!
If I get right to it
The job gets done
If I put it off
It don't!

Step Out

I can only walk
If I stand
I can only run
If I take a step
Whether I can see or not
I must step out
On God's promises

"The steps of a righteous man
Are ordered by the Lord"

"I will not leave you or forsake you"

"My grace is sufficient for you"

"Be not afraid"

"Only believe"

The Rocking Chair

I'm sitting here in my rocking chair
Which is supposed to mean I'm old
But those who haven't tried it
Don't know the pleasures it can hold

I go back to the days
I held my little babies in my arms
Hugged them tight and kissed them
And told them all their charms

When little toes were stepped on
And little tears streamed down their face
Nothing could comfort and heal them
Like mommy sitting and holding them
In this place
The rocking chair

God Does Things Different

If I knew what God was doing
Through His power in me
I'd climb the highest mountain
Walk on the deepest sea

But God does not always tell us
Or even let us see
He performs His work around us
And gives us victory

If I knew what God was doing
I might try to change it some
So I just hear and move with Him
He says
"My child, well done"

I Will

'I will' praise the Lord with my whole heart
'I will' lift up my hands in His Sanctuary
'I will' open my ears to hear His Word
'I will' use my feet to carry His Word
'I will' bless the Lord at all times
His praise will continually be in my mouth

'I will' hear the Lord
'I will' obey the Lord
'I will' have victory
'I will' walk in His ways
'I will' speak forth His praise to hearts in darkness

'I will' cause my heart to rejoice
'I will' rejoice in the valley
'I will' sing praises in the night
'I will' live the way God has directed me to live

My Strength Shall Be As My Day

As I look to the future
And wonder what it will hold
I seem to lose
The importance of this day
And the treasures it will hold

I am grateful for the sunrise
The little birds that sing
That I still live in a place
Where I can hear
The church bells ring

I feel the wind and hear the rain
I can sing and speak your name
I am blessed, Lord
And I am grateful
I will never be the same

Keep On Keeping On

I'm gonna keep on keeping on
Walking in faith and victory
No matter the circumstance
Wherever I be

To be whatever
He wants me to be
Without being puffed up
For others to see
I'm gonna keep on keeping on

Though dark may be the night
And the rain of affliction coming down
I'll walk in His spirit and presence
And be found
Keeping on!

Seek and Ye Shall Find

I looked for Jesus everywhere
And couldn't seem to find Him
Then I realized suddenly
That I couldn't see Him
Because He was
Snuggled in my heart

I will not fear what man
Shall do unto me
For I will look to the hills
From which cometh my help
The joy of the Lord is my strength
I will not falter or fail in Him!

The Lord Our God

The Lord our God
Has walked the path before us

The Lord our God
Has calmed the troubled sea

The Lord our God
Has surely gained the victory

The Lord our God
Will walk with you and me

Kindness

Kindness costs not one cent
But by it a soul
All twisted and bent
Was straightened and stood tall
And lived again in life anew
Because of the kindness
That came from you

Listening

I hear the rain drops
Spattering against the window
Falling softly, as if in
Reverence to the new day
All else is quiet
The space around me
Seems to be filled
With the knowledge
That God is close by
Waiting, listening for recognition
Knowing what the day holds for me
Ready to place it in my hands
To fill my heart again
With His glory and presence

Lord!

I want only your
Perfect will for my life
I am here today
So I will serve in
Whatever capacity
Or situation I am placed
I will arise in the morning
Go forth, at your direction
To do, to be, to cause
Things around me
To be different
The light will be brighter
The day more gentle
Because of your presence in me
I will hear and obey
And when I lay my head on my pillow
I will understand and know
I have walked today
In the perfect will of God!

These My Children, This My Child

I can't give them things I want to
In the realm of things to hold
But, I can give them things much better
Than the glitter and the gold

I can teach them love and patience
Faith in God, His work and plan
Give them great eternal values
Show them the good
Help them to stand

I can hold their hand in sorrow
Wipe the tears when things go wrong
Give them hope in darkest hours
Help them sing their happy song

I did birth them, I have led them
The best that I knew how
I'll be there forever for them
In the future, in the now

I'm their mother, and I do know
They have been loaned to me for awhile
So, I'll gladly love and hold them
These my children, this my child

Changes!

In the 'golden years'
Moms have a lot of time
To sit and think and pray
About their children and grandchildren
And anyone else who comes to mind

The things they have always wanted to do
Seems to have found a space
But they really aren't so important now
They have finally been put in their place

The eternal values of the soul
The lasting things of now
Things that will live on
After they are gone
Have risen up and taken charge
Their world is different somehow

His Presence In Me

I cannot take the long strides
That I did yesterday
Nor accomplish the weight lifting tasks
Of doing, going and always being there

But, I can take much smaller steps
Of being, going and doing
With the same love and compassion
The same care of loving and knowing

Lifting the cup of sorrow
Holding the hand of one, unsure
Smiling in the shadows
Patient with those who must endure

Walking more slowly
More of His glory I will see
And others will recognize more clearly
His presence in me

Afterward, You Shall Know

Your dreams and plans
All seem to have been swept away
Your hope, your faith
With fire is tried
The one who has walked beside you
And shared your every breath
Has walked on ahead of you
Their body cold in death

You look into your grief and pain
And cry that you may know
What is God doing now?
Why am I hurting so?

Then deep inside a voice speaks
So gentle and so low
"What I do now, thou knowest not
But afterward thou shall know"

Though the valley of death you walk
You'll reach the mountain crest
Your heart will sing with praise again
You've surely stood the test

You'll hear once more, that voice so clear
As it speaks as you onward go
"What I do now, thou knowest not
But afterward, thou shall know"

Waiting In The Shadows

There waits in the shadows
One, who has the map of our life in His hands
The years, months, weeks and days
According to His plans

We run hastily, here and there
Trying to find the way we should go
Asking, not waiting for answers
To the questions we speak
Of the things we want to know

While He stands quietly in the shadows
With the map in His hand
Waiting for us to be still
So He can give us His plan!

Be Still

Though I understand not this blessing
This trial of faith and will
I will wait and listen closely
To His voice "My child, be still"

Though I wish to move a mountain
I can't seem to find my place
I look everywhere around me
I can't seem to see His face

I know He has not left me
His promise is still the same
He will ever lead me onward
As I trust His mighty name

Somewhere midst all the thunder
And the waves that roar at will
I will hear again His speaking
"My child, My child, be still"

All In His Hand

Our worries are fruitless
Our fretting in vain
For God has it all in His hand

The mountain is the tallest
That we've ever seen
The bears in the wilderness
Ferocious and mean
But God has it all in His hand

The river is un-crossable
The storm clouds hang low
The hurricane is coming
We've no place to go
God has it all in His hand

There's nothing at all
That we can do
But pray and believe
And He'll see us through
For, God has it all in His hand

A Way For You

When the Egyptians have you surrounded
Stand tall and keep faith too
For by God's strong wind and power
He'll make a way for you

When the red sea is before you
And the enemy close behind
The mountains do surround you
You have no strength to climb

Take the 'rod' that God has given you
And follow close His plan
He will bring to you deliverance
As you obey and hold His hand

Ada Mae Harper

Things Aren't Always As They Seem

Sometimes we look at the mountains
They seem so tall
Impossible to climb
The rivers are at flood stage
There is no bridge
We're running out of time
'What is happening?' our hearts cry
We've no place to stand or lean

Then out of our soul
Comes the small quiet voice
"My child, things are not always as they seem
Trust me, not circumstances and things
I am your stairway, your bridge
Your place to lean
I'll take you to the top
I'll help you cross
I love you, My child, and remember
Things are not always as they seem"

Your Eyes On Him

If you're walking in your circumstances
With your eyes cast to the ground
They will certainly overcome you
And you will surely drown

Keep your eyes straight forth on Jesus
Walk on the water through the highest wave
And know, no matter what it looks like
He is there to save

As the storm seems to keep on raging
You will make it to a safe place
If you're not looking at the waters
But to His loving face

He has His arms around you
Holding you close to His heart
He will keep you, will not fail you
Keep your eyes up
Do your part

Life Is A Roadway

Life is a roadway traveling down through time
Sometimes it seems all up hill
And we feel too tired to climb

Our shoulders are aching
With the burdens we bear
And those around us
Don't seem to care

We forget that the burden bearer
Is walking at our side
In fact, He lives within us
To ever abide

Though our load may be heavy
Our future unsure
Jesus wants us to be free and happy
Not just to endure

If we worship Him continually
Take our moments, one at a time
Lay our heart's burden at His feet
The highest of hills we'll be able to climb

Where Do I Turn?

Lord, I don't know what to say
Or what to do
I feel that I'm floating
In space with you

My mind and body
Are in your control
I feel anxious, yet peaceful
Down in my soul

If I look at circumstances
There is no hope in sight
It's as if I'm walking
In the darkest of night

But I turn my eyes upward
See only you
I know, yes I know
You will show us what to do

The door that you've opened
Will come into view
We will be able
To walk right on through

No Need To Fight

Yea, though I walk through the valley
And the clouds hang low
Yea, though the storm is sure in coming
You will keep me, I know

Yea, in the heat of the summer
In the dark of the darkest night
I will hold your hand and be safe
The battle I won't need to fight

I will sing and march forth in your armor
Knowing I need not fear
I am, and will be, more than conqueror
For, The Captain of The Lord's Host is here!

Crushed

The fragrance of a flower comes forth
In the freshness of the morning
At the close of the day
At eventide

But when it is crushed
By some thoughtless footfall
It seems to break forth
In all of its glory
As it bleeds its fragrance
Into every corner and crevice
Of those who are near

৪৩

A man that asks

great things

Has great faith!

୫୦୦୪

I sowed my seed this morning.

I will harvest my crop in

its season.

ೋ ಌ

"Perfect Liberty"

My understanding:
Free to move with God,
In any area of our lives,
Without apology or fear
Of what others think.

Author Contact Information

Ada Harper
11 Lamar Street
Grenada, MS 38901

Phone: (662) 226-9101
E-mail: adaharper@bellsouth.net

Printed in the United States
45471LVS00002B/127-276